This is...

The Color **Black**

A book by Johnny O

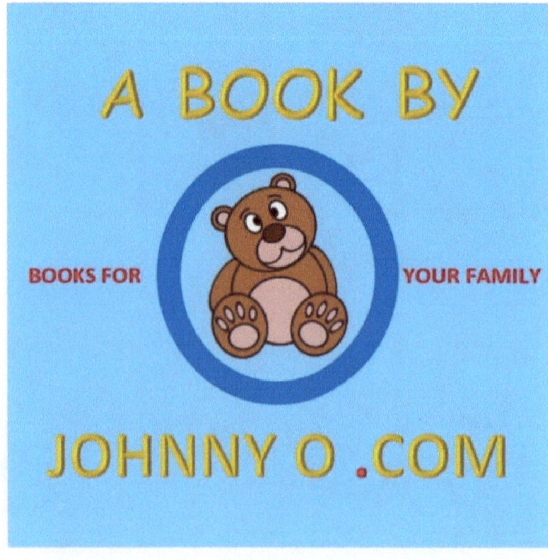
A BOOK BY
BOOKS FOR
YOUR FAMILY
JOHNNY O .COM

This is the color black

It can be seen in many places of your world

It can be seen on some of your clothes

such as this T-shirt

It can be seen on a car

such as this Maserati

or this sports car from Sweden

or this KTM X-Bow GT

built in Graz, Austria

Black can also be seen on some

road signs

like this one way road sign

or this keep right sign

or this speed limit sign

It lets you know the limit that
you can drive your car

It can be seen on some food you eat

such as these black olives

or these black raspberries

Commonly grown in the Pacific
Northwest part of the USA

Yummy, yummy

Black is the color of the roads we
drive on

such as this road

Black can also be the color of the
pepper you use for cooking meals

Black can even be a fun color

such as when you paint

or play with this balloon

Your TV remote may be black as well

Black can also be seen on some flowers

such as these Black Peony flowers

or these Black Hellebore flowers

Commonly called the Christmas
rose, it is poisonous and does not
belong to the rose family

Black can be seen on some
animals as well.

such as this Black Panther

this black bear

or this Arabian horse

Arabian horses were born in the Arabian Peninsula, Western Asia

The most common use for the color black is, the print in books

such as this book you are reading

This is...
The Color **Black**

About the Author

Good Day Everyone,

My name is John O'Connell and I write kids' books with no age limits.

The books I have written are books that inform not only the kids that read or hear them, but they also have a little information for the parents or guardians that read them to their child.

This allows you to see some general information that you may, or may have not known, and still be able to teach children about things they will encounter every day in their life and not have the constant question , of "what is that?", on their face.

These books will grow with your child as they grow.

As with all the books I write, I embed links that can give you more in-depth information, as you click on the photos.

I write to satisfy the basic needs of children, remembering what kinds of questions I had when I was young, so simply reading the book without clicking on the pics, can keep it simple for the younger children in your life.

As your child grows, they can click on the pictures, and that in return will give them more immediate information and a deeper knowledge of all the subjects I wrote about in the book you purchased. It is like getting a different book every time you turn the page.

These books will grow with your child through the years, giving them the eternal reward of knowledge

If you see or know a subject you would like me to write about, please feel free to email me and I will do my best to write a book concerning that subject and show them through pictures and facts, more about the world they are going to be entering into.

I am here to make the world a more positive and understandable world for the children, as well as help the parents or guardians teach their children about the basics, and if I can do that through a book that they can see actual pictures, basic terms, and facts, then I will do the best I can.

I THANK YOU for your support, and I am PROUD to be a part of your team and always remember, your child's learning, is an eternal reward

John O'Connell

Email: abookbyjohnnyo@gmail.com

Website: abookbyjohnnyo.com